Critical Comment on "Me First" and Ann Curran

"I think 'Me First' could have been a lot more obscure. It has too many punctuation marks, little Latin and no Sanskrit. But sometimes it made me LOL."

—James Joyce

"I haven't thought about her for years. Delightful, talented young woman! It's clearly evident in 'Me First.'"

—Gladys Schmitt

"I deny ever having met that woman."

—Hubert Humphrey

"As Thomas Aquinas said on his deathbed about the work of his lifetime, *'Videtur mihi sicut palea.'* [It looks like the stuff often found on stable floors.] I know Ann Curran. I know her work, and she is no Thomas Aquinas. Thank God."

—Jack Deedy

"Don't blame me. I just gave her the talent. Never told her what to do with it. However, I'm glad I made the cut."

—Jesus Christ

"I didn't like Ann Curran. She wasn't famous. She wasn't outrageous. She wasn't impressed with me at all."

—Andy Warhol

"I don't remember Ann Curran any more than she remembers me. But 'Me First' captures me, my accent and my beliefs in a surprisingly short space."
—Czeslaw Milosz

"No, we never discussed taking a bath together. Never took one either. But it's the thought that counts."
—Paul Mellon

"Who cares what a woman says?"
—Ludwig van Beethoven

"What a girl! I would have loved to take her on a horseback ride in Central Park. I could have explained Homestead to her."
—Andrew Carnegie

"Me? Frankly, I found her a bit snippy."
—Nancy Marchand

"If I had known Ann Curran, I would have loved her and taught her to climb a birch in her bare feet, how far up to boost herself, when to surrender and glide back to earth."
—Robert Frost

Me First

by
Ann Curran

ISBN 978-1-929878-44-4

First edition

PO Box 5301
San Pedro, CA 90733
www.lummoxpress.com

Printed in the United States of America

Acknowledgements

The author is grateful to the subjects of these poems, who willingly and sometimes unknowingly shared some portion of themselves and their lives with her; to Samuel Hazo, director of the International Poetry Forum, for his help in contacting most of the poets represented here; to the publications that assigned stories on some of these subjects, particularly "Carnegie Mellon Magazine," "Pittsburgh Magazine," "Pittsburgh Catholic," "The Pittsburgh Press" and "Pittsburgh Post-Gazette"; to the feisty Madwomen in the Attic at Carlow University; and to Rosaly DeMaios Roffman, Arlene Weiner and other members of the Squirrel Hill Poetry Workshop for their critical astuteness and support.

A thank you also to the following publications and websites for their earlier printing or audio presentation of these poems, several with slightly different titles:

"Me and the Fish Lady," "Me and Franco Harris and Lynn Swann," *Third Wednesday Magazine,* Fall, 2010
"Me and Seamus Heaney," *Rosebud Magazine*, Winter 2010/2011
"Me and Paul Mellon," *The Main Street Rag*, Summer 2011
"Me and Nancy Marchand," *The Main Street Rag*, Fall 2011
"Me and the Fish Lady," *Pittsburgh Post-Gazette*, April 14, 2012
"Me and Mary Weidner," *Voices from the Attic*, Vol. XVIII, 2012
"Me and Dorothy Day," *Pittsburgh Post-Gazette*, Nov. 17, 2012
"Me and a Photo Op," *Eye Contact,* Seton Hill University, Spring 2012
"Me and Domenic's Dictionary," *U.S. 1 Worksheets, Vol. 58, 2013*
"Me and Columbus and the Blubberers," "Me and Turkey," forthcoming, *Third Wednesday Magazine*
"Me and Kay Ryan," forthcoming, *The Main Street Rag*
"Me and Dorothy Day," *Her Circle*, hercircleezine.com, May 1, 2012
"Me and Imelda Tuttle," "Me and Andy Warhol," "Me and Paul Warhola," audio, *Hemingway's Poetry Series*, hemingwayspoetryseries.blogspot.com, Squirrel Hill Poetry Workshop, June 5, 2012
"Me and Buhl Planetarium," www.planetarium.cc/

Contents

III.

Contents *(continued)*

IV.

Foreword

Some of these poems, arranged roughly in chronological order, spring from interviews conducted for newspapers and magazines over several decades. They grew also from accidental and incidental contact with the rich and famous, the odd, the criminal, the extraordinary. These include Pittsburgh Steelers Franco Harris and Lynn Swann, philanthropist and art connoisseur Paul Mellon, Nobel laureates Seamus Heaney, Czeslaw Milosz, and Herbert Simon, presidential candidate Barack Obama, Vice President Hubert Humphrey, and an Artificial Linguistic Internet Computer Entity named A.L.I.C.E. Other poems emerged from the poet's personal universe. Special thanks to childhood chum Diane Yeagley, my first real boss, Jack Deedy, Dorothy Day, my husband, Ed Wintermantel, our daughter, Cristin Curran Wintermantel, and son-in-law, Christopher Buckley, my sister, Mary Patricia Curran, and, of course, Jesus Christ.

I.
"Run, Ann. Run."

—Diane Yeagley

Me and Diane Yeagley

meander home from St. Anselm School.
First-graders hungry for something sweet,
we pause in the bowling alley, look for
unretrieved change in the telephone booth.
We ask some guy for a dime. He says, "Sure.
Follow me." We go along Noble Street
to the tracks. Then I am alone heading
toward the dark underpass. He turns toward
me yards away. He stops. I stop. Something
hangs from his pants. I freeze, confused, then jarred
by Diane's screech from on high: "Run, Ann. Run,"
echoing our readers. I hear the fear
in her voice and bolt up the soot-soft hill.
My shoes fill with coal dust,
my memory with dirt.

Me and Family Secrets

You don't always know those you think you know.
It creeps out at death. Candy in pockets,
in drawers, all the purses, bedside tables,
and I never saw Aunt Maggie eat it.

Thomas with his naked-girl magazines
hidden as though his mother might find them
and him living alone for years by now.
Jimmy with his down-and-dirty photos

in a pouch with a roach clip in his den,
five copies of "A Vast Conspiracy,"*
about Clinton's sins, in the living room.
Cupboards full of fast-food death for his heart.

And me? What have I stashed away to tell
some sad, ugly story about my life,
some secret I no longer care about
or, thank God, cannot even remember?

* *"The Real Story of the Sex Scandal That Nearly
Brought Down a President" by Jeffrey Toobin. The
book's back-cover promo says it "brings a dignity and
integrity to the story that it has never before received."*

Me and My First Bishop

The bishop checked my report card
for the American Legion
which gave me a college scholarship
because my Daddy had ruined
his life fighting in World War I.
Now we know: no one gets over that.

The bishop said, "You got an 'A'
in logic and you're a woman."
He thought that was rather funny.
I didn't get the joke at all.
He didn't review my grades again.
The Dean of Women handled that.

Me and Gladys Schmitt

hit it off in her living room.
Me, a sophomore reporter.
She, a successful novelist.
Built like a long-limbed spider,
she stretches arms across the sofa
with great drama. A cigarette smolders
between two fingers. She sips a
drink. Crawford without the bitchy streak.
"My husband is translating 'The Iliad'
in a compromise hexameter."
I hold back a laugh and quiz her on writing.
"Maybe you would come and read
some of my drafts?" she urges.
A foolish, flattering request.
But somehow it frightens me.

I entertain my family
for months with imitations of her:
arms wave, she inhales the cigarette,
makes obscure literary comments.
It earns me the nickname "Gladys"
from my favorite brother.
That evolves to "Glad-Ass,"
"Happy Bottom," then the staid "Hap."

Years later, I meet her students,
Carnegie Tech alumni:
writers, producers, directors,
all glistening with success.
To them she was the main gemstone
of their education, shining still,
illuminating all the questions
never asked in class but always
kicked around in her living room.

Me and JFK

For Gov. David L. Lawrence

So young, so handsome, so articulate.
so Irish, so Catholic, so humorous.
Somehow we had all reached the top with him.
My first president. I went door-to-door
for him, reported to a consulate
around the corner, adored Camelot.
When I berated David L. Lawrence
for not supporting Kennedy, he said
he knew what being Catholic had cost him
when he ran for governor of our state.

I never in my heart lost faith in him
even when Camelot grew uglier
than the original. I stood sobbing
in my living room as his caisson rolled by.
His widow veiled in black, his two babies,
his brothers stricken in their morning suits,
de Gaulle and other greats moving on foot
down Pennsylvania Avenue. Crowds hushed,
still wounded by those bullets in Texas.

Me and Buhl Planetarium

The Van de Graaff generator always sparks
excitement at Buhl Planetarium.
An aide, I put my hand to that silver ball.
The sting startles. My hair rises. I touch kids,
pass the shock years before our microwaved world.
We play with fire and ignore it for the kick.
Buhl ejects me from my white, Catholic orbit.
I gain a black buddy with gorgeous green eyes,
humor that lightens dark days. A Jewish guy

who wants to date me like I want to date him
is engaged to a Jewish girl. That was that.
Upstairs in the observatory, I shrink
before dark sun spots captured on a white disk.
I am stunned to prayer by Saturn and its rings.
The Foucault pendulum hypnotizes all
as it moves back and forth, across the pit floor.
Won't it ever strike down the next pin in the pit?
When I tell the story, I get halfway through—
stumble on the free-swinging wire, Earth's movement—

no longer believe a word of what I've said.
The aides spend hours repairing Science Fair
exhibits. Small hands ignore do-not-touch signs.
The glue dries, the Scotch tape gives way, things fall loose.
The biggest thrill for planetarium aides:
the Sky Show in the Theater of the Stars.
It runs all day. People sit in this round globe
of a room. Lights dim. The Zeiss projector lifts
slowly from the floor like an alien ship.

It splatters the walls with stars and galaxies.
A disembodied voice takes us beyond Earth.
Meanwhile, two aides slip into silver costumes
go out on the catwalk behind the curved walls.
The voice snaps on our lights. We play astronauts.
We confer. Shake our heads yes. Shake our heads no.
Shrug maybe. Click switches. Study our checklists.
We pretend that all is under our control
as we wing through space and the commanding voice
tells the piddling bit we know of the universe.

Me and Jack Deedy

He came to town with Bishop Wright,
who liked to strut around the streets
in scarlet skull cap and cassock.
They argued by phone every week
when the "Pittsburgh Catholic" published.

But Mr. Deedy—"Call me Jack"—
 gave me good assignments—mostly.
"Go to the museum and find
something Christian to write about."
I shrank below Ghiberti's doors,
gem of the Florence Baptistry:
scripture aglow in bronze relief
long before the Bible nestled
blushing in bedside motel drawers.
"Meet Dorothy Day at Mount Mercy.
See what she has to say and why."
I discovered pure compassion.
"Know some French? Interview that priest
from New Guinea…can't speak English."
I soon learned my limitations.

He taught me to sweat the details.
Asked no more than he did of himself.
Write, rewrite, proof, then proof again.
Check, double-check. He liked my work.

I followed him to daily Mass.
He crossed his arms across his chest
to receive Holy Communion.
Moved on to the national scene
with left-leaning "Commonweal"
still pushing his slow-moving church
toward its original mission.

Me and The Choice

I could have married a Pepsi salesman
from New Mexico if I played my cards
right or if I knew I had any cards
or if I didn't prefer Coke instead.

I could have married the sweetest gay guy
if he'd asked me and I remained stupid
about everything related to sex
and dismissed the ugly bits of gossip.

I could have married a glum Italian
if I'd opted for money and not love
or if his plush music room seduced me
or if he were a few inches taller.

But I married you, a tall, beer drinker,
more maddeningly male than my brothers,
yet able to spell and wander in words,
able to hold me with a fierce, kind heart.

Me and Jesus Christ

go a way back. Before I remember.
Maybe when my heart started to beat.
I was so afraid of his church
I confessed adultery believing
it was pretending to be an adult.
He understood. Sent me to his mother.
God, he was crazy about that woman.
The only perfect human being
besides himself, and he had advantages.
She became my direct line, a sure thing.
Just ask. She gave sort of slanted answers.
But they were there. Clear as the clouds of doubt.

Then, the Trinity. I didn't truck much
with the Father. Why did Christ call him that
if God has no sex? Simple enough:
so we dumbos would get it. God's idea
of herself was so perfect, it bloomed
into an exact image. The mother,
the daughter, the father, the son.
Only one fit in the first century.

Then there was the Bird,
formerly known as the Holy Ghost,
upgraded now to the Holy Spirit.
That Bird flew between that perfect pair
carried absolute love for each other.
That divine dove was no more a bird
than God was a mother or a father.
That Bird could wing its way into your heart
bringing more joy than you can grasp or bear.
You'd find yourself thanking God for the Bird.
Jesus would say, "OK, OK, OK, I heard."

For Rev. Gordon Knight, C.S.Sp.

Me and Turkey

We tramp through morning sun and dusty roads
to sit on a tight row of stone toilets

in Ephesus where St. Paul did business.
We hear about the secret passageway

from the library to the whorehouses.
The men were afraid of God or their wives.

The bus dips down to the rug company
and I learn the Turks make Orientals.

They flip them in the air to present them
at our feet: a flying carpet landing.

Then off to Mary's House. A Romanesque
brick building, where the mother of God lived.

Yes, the mother of Jesus Christ Himself.
We sing "Hail Holy Queen Enthroned Above,"

pray a single Hail Mary and move on.
Some write petitions on bits of white cloth

and tie them on a wall below the house.
Like flags, they lift and mutter in the air.

The building looks so fresh, I have to ask.
"Built in 1954," Sister says.

Me and Dorothy Day

meet for coffee and watery soup
at a downtown five-and-dime lunch counter.
Me, a cub reporter; she, a wise woman.
I know she picketed the White House,
demanded the vote, went to jail, escaped
with a presidential pardon. She left
her lover for her religion. I know
she started a string of Houses
of Hospitality for the homeless
and unemployed. They still have no vacancies.

In her kitchen, she cooked up the radical
"Catholic Worker," fought for peace, did penance
for Hiroshima and Nagasaki.
I know her church forgave her an abortion,
but she never forgave herself. I know
Notre Dame gave her the Laetare Medal
for "comforting the afflicted
and afflicting the comfortable."
To me, she preaches her gospel at the counter,
the kind of place where civil rights began.

(Yes, she worked that row, too.) She fished her clothes
from donation barrels and today looks like
a Scandinavian queen in a knit hat
sprinkled with silver bangles,
a halo on one now rising toward sainthood.
All I recall of our conversation:
"That extra coat in your closet
belongs to the person with none."
She left a mark on me that day.
Every winter I give away a coat,
ashamed to own more than one at a time.

*"Don't call me a saint. I don't want to be
dismissed so easily."—Dorothy Day*

Me and the Catholic Bishops
For Pope Francis I, S.J.

The bishops are selling their mansions.
In Pittsburgh Bishop David Zubik moves
into a seminary apartment.
He gives up the fine art and antiques in
the thirty-nine room house with five-car garage,
breakfast nook, butler's pantry, Wuerlpool tub.
Just the taxes run $44,000.
Why? Penance for the pedophile priests' sins.
Shifted around but never charged or jailed.
Never placed out of reach of the children.
Who will light the ten fireplaces, restock
the wine cellar, teach young priests to tend bar?
Where will they entertain the next George Bush
when he calls weeks before the election?
The house sold for $1.74 million, a real deal.

It looked like one man's form of repentance.
Now, the archbishops are selling their mansion.
The stone Victorian Gothic pile
where Philadelphia archbishops lived
since 1935 is up for sale.
Former home to archbishops and four red hats.—
yes, the cardinals are selling their mansion—
the house had welcomed Pope John Paul II,
President Reagan and his astrologer.
They've promised the proceeds to inner-city
parishes. The house has sixteen rooms, five
baths, granite walls, slate roofs, on eight acres.
Don't know the price. If you have to ask, don't.
The archbishop may choose to live beside
the cathedral in a rectory built
for archbishops when they were less royal.
It's all so sudden and quite delightful—
as though Luther had risen from the dead
still stunned by the opulence of old Rome.

Me and Brendan Kennelly*

Brendan Kennelly's cousin Ted married
my cousin Mina in Ballylongford.
Ted worked at the creamery and cut hair
in the kitchen. Mina swept up after him.

Kennelly wrote an odd book of poems
about Oliver Cromwell and his feats.
He looked at savagery by Prods and Micks.
(We once named our goofiest dog "Cromwell.")

My good friend Pat Dolan met Kennelly
in a Listowel pub. They disagreed
on a point of poetry, and he dumped
a pitcher of Guinness over her head.

*Kennelly is an Irish poet, novelist, former professor
at Trinity College, Dublin. He titled one of his poems
"Poetry My Arse."*

Me and Bill Cosby

He leans against the tennis club wall, waits
for his partner. I gasp. This comedian
digs his laughs out of the ordinary,
takes us inside his family, shows us
how human and dumbly they can behave.
We see ourselves in him, his kids, his wife.
Just google Chocolate Cake for Breakfast
and you'll understand. I was thrilled silly
to meet this genius. I could do no more
than rave about his recent Jell-O ad.

Me and Franco Harris and Lynn Swann

play tennis at the same club.
Me, a B-minus player.
They, sterling Pittsburgh Steelers.
One day those Pro Football Hall of Famers
helped me win a key match
simply by being there, right on the next court
in all their good-looking glory
totally distracting my opponent.
All I noticed was two hard hitters,
but she couldn't keep her eyes
on the ball, missing my wimpiest shots.
Me and those guys with eight Super Bowl rings
beat the crap out of that ditzy dame,
and I became the Round Robin Runner Up.

Me and My Sister

My sister saves strays:
spiders, pesky bugs
that invade her space.

I execute them
with bare hands, my shoe,
death by flushed toilet.

She says arachnids
eat bad bugs, swallow
one hundred a day.

Spiders—black widows,
tarantulas—won't
hurt us—usually.

Spiders are the start
of her sweet rescues.
When rain brings curled worms

to the tennis court,
we open papers
to suck up puddles,

swing brooms and squeegees
while my sister lifts
stranded, writhing worms,

and kindly hauls them
back to the soaked ground
they had abandoned.

Me and Jack Klugman

"Interviewing is not a spectator sport."
—George Anderson, Drama Critic,
 "Pittsburgh Post-Gazette"

It was the worst interview ever.
Except the time when the Bulgarian
ambassador ran his hand up and down
my back while I stood asking him questions.
A university moneygrabber comes
with actor Jack Klugman and inhibits

the one-on-one connection that allows
real responses instead of packaged PR.
She interrupts his answers as they start
to bloom into his genuine beliefs.
She tries to reply to questions for him.
She inserts her own shallow comments

as though *she* is the point of our meeting.
Mostly Klugman cries about the great cost
of buying, feeding, training race horses,
intent on underlining his poverty.
He feels her hands in his pockets and soul.
He can't leave the restaurant soon enough.

Me and Imelda Tuttle

When she tells Andy Warhola she lives
in McKeesport, he loves the name and boasts
to Carnegie Tech friends that he lives there,
too. Not in a slim, yellow brick row house
for Slovak immigrants in South Oakland.
After graduation, she visits Warhol
in New York. He shows her his first soup cans.

"What are you doing?" she shrieks in horror.
"Don't worry, Mel. This will work. You just watch."
Before long his Manhattan factory blooms
with celebrity faces: Marilyn,
Jackie, Dolly Parton start with photos.
Just like the art he stuck up on the walls
of his childhood sickroom: Hollywood stars
clipped from newspapers, movie magazines
down on Dawson Street near culture central.

*

She has a good heart and two fuzzy dogs.
Their kinky hair looks like her kinky hair.
She brings pumpkin pie to the faculty
at Pittsburgh's first community college.
Some don't notice the crinkled light whatzits
suspended squiggling in the baked pumpkin.
Some do and declare it shaved coconut.
A few know there are only three suspects.

Me and Imelda teach English. Today,
we'll talk about the coward: passive voice.
Students scrawl an example on the wall:
"Annie Oakley is fucked." The subject does
not perform the action found in the verb.
Imelda, with no eye for that pie, can't hide
a first step toward her final dementia.

Me and Tony O'Reilly

meet on the telephone before cells. Back
when he could say his wife was Australian.
Well before her Greek successor drove him
to buy the Jackie Onassis diamond ring.

Somehow, someone convinced his country, Ireland,
to send tons of great, ancient treasures to town.
Like the Vatican shipping the Pieta
to a former marsh/garbage dump in Queens
for viewing from a quarter of a mile away.
O'Reilly, once a world-class rugby player,
now head of Heinz, kicks off the local show.

He returns my call while three preschoolers
dance like the crazed in my kitchen/office.
He sprinkles food words—peppered, relish—
though he is not talking about edibles.
We discuss the Cross of Cong, once possessed
by Turlough O Conor, king of Connacht,
in the 12th century. It holds a relic
of the true cross. O'Reilly says he comes
from a long line of devout clergymen.
We laugh at the implications of that.

He doesn't mention that family abbots
may have worked on the Book of Kells
with its convoluted, colorful world.
Yes, monks drank beer. No, it wasn't Guinness.
In the end, O'Reilly says I should come
to the show. I don't tell him that I would
have to sell this story twice to buy
one ticket to Treasures of Early Irish Art.

Me and Hubert Humphrey

find each other alone
in a Hilton back hallway.
I didn't know much about him
except he was the man who might
have been president instead
of Tricky Dick. I approach him
to introduce myself as
a fan. I think he thought
I was a novice bimbo
in my tailored suit and low heels.
He eyes me up and down,
with a slight sneer. Perhaps
a Minnesota put-down.
I was stunned decades before
Monica Lewinsky flipped
her thong at Bill Clinton.

Me and the Vestibule

"Write about your vulva," the teacher directs.
All the wrinkled poets giggle but comply.
Biology class never got specific.
But they've learned one thing terrific through research.
The front door—down there—is called the vestibule
of the vagina like the entrance to church.
They like to think of it as a holy place.
Their creations—Jake, Emma—started right there.

Then look at those chubby folds of labium,
making "a nice, warm place"…for the penis,*
the cleavage in between, the cleft, the slit.
Don't forget the urethra, the pee place.
And then the special spot, one step to heaven.
Call it clit, clitoris, the magic button,
"an organ homologous to the penis."
Press that button! Press that button! Press that button!

* *Wikipedia to the rescue*

Me and Mister Rogers

"I can't put that word in
Santa Claus's mouth."
—Herb Stein, Editor, Pittsburgh Magazine

And so, are you good in bed,
Mister Rogers? the writer said.
Two sad sons and a glum wife
hint at some sorrow in your life.
Or to rephrase, do you drink?
Kahlua in coffee, you think?
Is there something, sir, some fault,
do you cheat at cards, assault
children in the neighborhood,
do things because they aren't good?
Show us some sign you are real.
Show us some sign that you feel
grim, dumb, nasty or anything
but eternal cheer; that you
hate cardigans, tennis shoes,
pushy toddlers, snotty tots;
that, in fact, you say "shit" a lot.
That the preacher did admit.
No one, however, believed it.

II.
"The history of my stupidity could fill thirty volumes."

—Czeslaw Milosz

Me and Mary Weidner

snicker about her chicken pictures.
They began in an open-air market
in Montmartre. She snapped photos
of the Eiffel Tower, Notre Dame,
then slipped around a corner and found
plucked chickens and turkeys dangling,
lined up, piled up for purchase.
The artist knows when she trips upon her subject.
Les Poulets Parisiennes were born

on film, in oil, watercolor, pencil.
She knows they won't sell, these sensuous
but something-more-than-naked chickens.
They resemble human body parts,
skin like yours or mine, not fowl.
Curves suggest people's private parts.
"Is that obscene?" my naïve self asks.
"It could be interpreted that way," she says.

Me and Watfa Midani

A colorful mishmash of the half-naked
in blue, green, scarlet, tan, brown, ghostly white.
Two panels, four birds—one, upside down.
Watfa, the painter, calls it "The Swimmers."
Arms reach overhead, float in the blue-black,
all "squiggly" as she saw them underwater.

Big breasts bared in panel one. A strange red
figure appears on both sides. The artist's
spouse, an enigmatic dean of fine arts,
calls the painting "The Judgment of Paris."
A guy must pick the fairest of three goddesses.
They offer lovely bribes: wealth and power,

glory in battle, love. Aphrodite
flashes a breast, predicts Helen of Troy.
She wins. The others retaliate with
ten lousy years of the Trojan War. And death.
No wonder that sweet bird flips upside down.
"Swimmers," Watfa insists. "In water. Swimmers."

Me and Nancy Marchand

walk across campus at what she calls Carnegie Tech.
Me: a public relations drone.
She: a famous actress yet to play the "monster mother"*
of mobster Tony Soprano on HBO.
Someone with an eye on her fame and purse
convinced her to come home to her alma mater.

Queen of "the wise and imperious authority figures,"
she shone as Lady Sneerwell in "The School for Scandal,"
as the nun, who prompted hysterical laughter
from guilt-ridden, cradle Catholics
in "Sister Mary Ignatius Explains It All for You,"
and inevitably as the wicked stepmother in "Cinderella."

My job: walk her to the College of Fine Arts
where she honed her skills for measured meanness
and down-her-nose uppity dismissiveness.
I tell her about the long and careful job
of cleaning the exterior of this Hornbostel gem,
a 3-D piece of art to inspire the blooming artists.

It was a building dusted with the black dirt of decades
in the polluted air of the steel capital of Pittsburgh.
She pulls herself up tall, stiffens, curls that lower lip
and spits out her take on the shining white edifice:
"I liked it better dirty!" Class dismissed.
We complete our walk in silence.

* Based on "The New York Times" Nancy Marchand
obituary

Me and Domenic's Dictionary

Sundays before Mass, the choir practices
in Mrs. Gannon's bright fifth-grade classroom.

I sit at Domenic's desk and borrow
his eraser, flip through his dictionary:

"The Best Dictionary for Students."
The front cover says, "Knowledge is Power,"

quoting Francis Bacon in 1620.
I check what's missing: vagina, penis.

There will be no action in this small book.
The editors allow a female egg

but no sperm, though there's a bride and bridegroom.
Don't look for poop, shit or fornication.

Breast made the cut as "two parts on the front
of a woman's body that can give milk."

Maybe Dom will get an upgrade next year—
a sixth-and-seventh-graders' appendix.

In my seventh grade, one girl got pregnant.
I doubt the dictionary did it though.

Me and Judith Resnik

fulfill one of her "two PRs a month"
before she leaves Earth as an astronaut.
She has promise written all over her.
Perfect SAT score, valedictorian.
She switches from math to engineering
because she wants to make real things happen.
She's the second U.S. woman in space
and the first American Jew. "It's not
important who's first. It is important
that we each get an opportunity."

She circles the globe ninety-six times.
Up in Florida, down in California.
She activates a solar wing used today
to light and operate the space station.
She shimmies the launch of three satellites
for communications. Maybe the one
that sends GPS directions to you.
"It was great, and I'm ready to go back,"
she exclaims after a perfect landing.

And back she goes in 1986,
with six doomed others on Challenger.
It breaks apart in about a minute
and rains shock and sorrow around the world.
She earns a NASA Space Flight Medal of Honor.
Schools name a dorm and a lab after her.
Someone calls a crater on the far side
of the moon "Resnik." She looked like a bride,
all innocence, posed in her white space suit.
In weightlessness, she laughed as her dark curls
rose above her. She was just thirty-six.

Me and Remembrance

It was a Day of Remembrance
on campus. For fifteen minutes
each would read the names of the dead.
Those railroaded to the death camps:
Jews, Poles, Russians, the disabled,
homosexuals, criminals,

Social Democrats, Communists,
intelligentsia, lawyers,
priests, nuns, ministers of all stripes.
Anyone Hitler pointed to.
An 11-million death toll.
I could read names. I *should* read names.

Turns out, we read birth and death dates,
and my list was all little kids:
Eta Halberstam, two months old
Ytzkhak Ajzenman, one year old
Emanuil Prus, two years old
Abraham Jacob, three years old

Gabor Neumann, four years old
I could do the math easily.
I could taste horror. I could not
complete my fifteen-minute list.
I failed remembrance. We all do.

Me and a Hero

His favorite war story stunned
everyone who heard about it.
He helped evacuate the last
skeletal prisoners from Dachau.
"For a joke," he bragged, in mid-flight

he opened the cockpit door
and tossed empty beer bottles
down the aisle. He roared about
what the passengers must have thought.
When he died, an old man without

a memory of anything,
the Army buried him with full
military honors. Taps
with its twenty-four sorry notes
brought tears to everyone's eyes.

Me and Herb Simon

never talked economics or game theory.
He loved to explain the games he played,
the mechanical puzzles that stumped him.
I first met him because my nervous boss
was aghast over a proposed photo
of Simon, a daddy of artificial intelligence,
shown with a motherboard in his head,
a composite by our clever photo guy.
Simon settled the question quickly.
With a quiet, "You guys are the artists,"
he handed the magazine cover back.

For Bill Redic, photographer

Me and Barbara Bosson

ride the Monongahela Incline
together, with her son in tow.
Me: a magazine editor.
She: neurotic, whining, wacky
Fay Furillo of "Hill Street Blues."
Back in the car, the kid plays
with my daughter's math flashcards.
When I drop them off, he exits,
numeral drills in hand. I remind
him to leave them behind.

At lunch, we join Dad,
Steven Bochco, who eats a hearty
cafeteria plate. Barbara munches
on a couple of lettuce leaves.
Later she complains about a headache.
He says, quite straight-faced,
"It must have been that big lunch."

When I write the story
I double-check her stint
as a Playboy Bunny. She asks
that I leave that out. I do
to appease the fundraisers.
Carnegie Mellon then names her
—its first Playboy Bunny—
to the sedate board of trustees.
And why not? She is
among the five percent
of the nation's working actors.
Her guy is Croesus* in overdrive.

*Croesus, a fifth century B.C. king of Lydia, was
famous for his wealth. "Rich as Croesus" or "richer than
Croesus" are still common references in English.

Me and My Present

When the Children's Home
gave us our daughter,
they held her on high—
a round, pink person,
bow scotch-taped to head,
face asking what's this?
A present, I thought.
Today I recalled the scene
when she phoned with
sweet birthday wishes:
gift from a present.

Me and Maxine Kumin

tangle minds on the telephone.
Me, a freelance writer.
She, a Pulitzer Prize-winning
poet and horse breeder.
What's she most proud of?
"Oh, Lord!" Stunned that writing
made a life for her. Proud
of her "long and successful marriage."
They're competitive trail riders.
Pleased with all three kids.
Happy about the horses
galloping through their lives;
willing to shovel their manure.
She and her husband grow veggies
out of granite on their New Hampshire farm.
They tap the sweetness out of maples.
A lovely Frostian image.

Changes in her time? Women writers
"are getting published. They don't
have to hide behind their first initial."
The retreat from formal patterns.
Sinking into the confessional.
"*Moi, moi, moi* all over the place
but ebbing a bit." Advice?
"For God's sake, read poems.
They write poems but don't read poems."
The Pulitzer didn't hurt her.
She "advanced from a nobody at all"
to "at least somebody." More readings,
more job offers. U.S. poet laureate.
But yes, the general public still sees
the poet as a "fop or buffoon,
absent-minded, head in the clouds."

Me and a Photo Op

Somebody ought to catch that moon,
a great white globe with aura
wider than itself, trapped, tangled
in a crisscross of tree branches
sitting above a hill of white
houses painted by its last light.
Not me. My battery is dead.

Me and the Ax-Killer

agree to meet at the prison.
There is really no other option.
Me, a university magazine editor.
He, not a distinguished alum.
But in prison he blossomed, became
more than a bright mechanical engineer.
Wrote three books of poetry, seduced
a grant from the National Endowment
for the Arts, founded the Academy
of Prison Arts, even got married.
Not enough? Earned an English/psych
degree *magna cum laude*. My favorite:
he engineered a new door for the prison
and didn't use it as an exit.

The guards set me up in a huge yellow room.
I plug in the tape recorder. Then alarmed,
see the wire as a weapon.
Never trusted batteries. Take a chance.
He comes in quietly—a blond guy with glasses.
Quite slight. Would have had to use
his brains to survive inside.
I would guess he seldom smiles.
He certainly doesn't this day.
He probably never laughs.
Strung tight enough to break in two.

We don't get specific on the murder.
How he climbed a trellis
to his former fiancée's bedroom.
found her sleeping, took an ax to her.
Her mother rushed in, saw the worst.
Then he begins to destroy her again
chopping with words, justifying the murder,

explaining his anger with a reason.
I'll give it—and his name—no space.
We correspond for a time.
I start to worry about his release.
Most murderers kill once, a terrible
volcanic burst of fiery feeling.
But this guy is so cool,
like a giant icicle doomed
to fall and cut through flesh.

Me and Ruth Stone

One little piggy haunts Ruth Stone.
She sees him cross the road, dragging hind hooves.
She calls the humane society.
They take him away. "I feel terrible
about it," she says, regret catching her voice

on the phone from her mountain in Vermont,
where the evergreen woods fill up with snow
and the moon sets her dark world all aglow.
She wishes she had been a wise parent,
a more loving daughter, had learned much more.

But women "close their eyes in happiness."
She doesn't mention her husband. I ask.
"He thought we were twins. He's still part of me.
He murdered himself. It cut me in two."
She raised their daughters alone, "terribly poor."

Poetry paid for plumbing, a new roof.
"I love to ride buses," she says, about
one of her sources of inspiration.
Beet field workers, bicyclists talk to her.
"One of the good things about poetry:

You don't know what's in that great darkness
in your head until you start to do it."
When did poetry begin for her?
As her mother nursed her, she read Tennyson's
"In Memoriam" aloud. Ruth drank in meter and milk.

Me and Czeslaw Milosz

I'll level with you. I don't recall
diddly of my phone conversation
with Nobel laureate Czeslaw Milosz
almost a quarter of a century ago.
I sense a kindness and wisdom in him
and I treasure my tape-recording
of our talk and listened to it twice.
There were two garbled sections. Nothing like
Nixon's eighteen-minute Watergate gap.

He was a man from another world.
The Poland he represented in Paris
made him vomit. He couldn't stand the game
of chess that left no possible move
on either side. He saw communism
bloom out of the dead Christian faith
of the Russian intelligentsia—
an ism "indifferent to good and evil."

He adapted to California,
its huge deserted, dry areas.
"The Great Republic, moderately corrupt.
That's much better than totally corrupt,"
he assures. "Any reality
has a certain dose of corruption."
Somehow he works in how he has grown.
"The history of my stupidity
would fill thirty volumes," he confides.
Every new revelation uncovers
the darkness of his previous vision.

At home, he says, "I am very hot potato,
a writer who doesn't hide his opinion."
The underground Catholic press prints his work.
"You're a Catholic?" "Yes."
"You're a Catholic?" "Yes."
We discover a bit of common ground.
He teaches Slavic lit at Berkeley,
writes poems, engages "in a very strange
occupation here in California"—
translating Old and New Testament books
from Hebrew and Greek into Polish.
He lives long enough for Poland to change
and then goes home to die in Krakow.

Me and Allen Ginsberg
and One of the Clancy Brothers

All I remember
on the downside
of memory:
a bright spring day
two back-to-back
phone interviews:

Allen Ginsberg
and his "best minds,"
beatnik buddies,
dumbed dead with dope.
He, boring, bored.

Someone Clancy
fresh, funny
storyteller
the brogue I love.
Just no contest.

Me and Andy Warhol

I didn't want to interview him.
A creepy old guy, hanging with weirdos.
The twisted photographer insisted.
Off we went with some purist art pupils
to The Factory and this blushing success.
We check out his workout spot with girly weights,
watch him react to the scorn of students,
conduct a brief interview on the way
out the door as he constructs a wall
with monosyllabic yeses and noes
to hide the person he is, was, will be:
an enigma all the way to the grave
on a cold Castle Shannon hillside
littered with soup cans and Brillo boxes.

Me and Paul Warhola

He hikes up to my garret
where squirrels and bats drop by
along with bees and sunshine.
A big, gruff, scrap-dealer guy,
born in Slovakia,
oldest brother of Andy Warhol
who had dropped his final "a."
He brings a story and gift:
his Absolut Warhola ad.
He signs it with a last "a"
that stands alone. Made five breaks

in his name. Leaves one in mine.
Creative. Big-ego caps.
His signature chicken feet
compete with rows of vodka.
A photograph duped three times.
Six brothers stare out at me.
Andy stands like taller Paul
but tilts his head to the right.
Paul says he didn't just die.
An unknown *they* murdered him.
I forget the dire motive.

Me and My Genes

My genes remember sitting by the fire
where they listened to mind-binding ghost tales
or mysteries raising goose bumps, neck hair.

Sometimes, someone told a knee-slapping joke,
but they often saved those for the next wake.
Gram laid out in bed behind the fireplace

in that chilly stone cottage in Galway
or Kerry. Who can escape their nature?
On cold evenings when dark descends, I sit

before my warm, glowing Panasonic.
Stories always start with a dead body
and I drag my past forward yet again.

Me and Seamus Heaney

talk across the Atlantic Ocean before his Nobel.
Me, perched on my bed beside the only phone
that hooks up to my tape recorder.
He, "beside the waters of Dublin Bay,"
already bootless and knee-deep in poet talk.

A cagey guy, he learned early how to hedge
growing up Catholic in Orange territory.
Even wrote about a boyhood buddy
killed by the Royal Ulster Constabulary
without mentioning who did the deed.
His excuse: they were "off duty…two bad apples."
A nicely altered cliché. He's thinking.
He knew readers would blame the I.R.A.
He teeters atop the stonewall, appeasing Prods.

He lives at Harvard or in Ireland,
where taxi drivers chat him up about his poetry.
People approach him in the local pub.
Not like the ivory tower U.S. poets.
Frankly, he charms me for forty-five minutes
with stories and beliefs wrapped in a green brogue.
As we close, I say my contact wants him to do more press.
His instant anger sizzles across the sea.
"You tell him, I think I've done enough for him."
That clearly included my grilling. Ouch!
The distance between us suddenly expands
wider than the waters of the Atlantic.

III.
"Enough about me. Let's talk about my blue dress."

—A.L.I.C.E.

Me and Paul Mellon

rank a warm bath
as one of life's greatest gifts.
(Not together, of course.)
Easing into the steaming water,
closing the shower door
to hold the heat inside,
snuggling down with a magazine
that takes occasional quick dips,
reaching up with toes
to twist the H spigot again.

For me, a joy to match the sun
igniting a million diamonds on snow.
For him, a rival to a rotating parade
of treasured masterpieces
borrowed from his storehouse
and hung in his own home gallery.
The ultimate one-man show.
That painted line separates us.
Maybe our soap choices do, too.

Me and EU Therapy

The tub becomes a great lime pond
called Juniper Spruce Herbal Bath.
I slosh it into bubble clouds
that break apart. Their shadows bruise
my thighs like real clouds seen from on high
leave telltale spots on water, land.

A soothing EU therapy
made in Dresden that we bombed
into windowless half-buildings,
killing few soldiers, just people.
Sunk down in this steamy, hot bath
I remember the cold, stone house

my grandfather left in Ireland.
No tub, toilet, running water.
Why not sail to a new country
where your spoiled offspring can collapse
in juniper berry, spruce oil?
Wouldn't that be better for all?

Me and Andrew Carnegie

always knew each other.
He was the little blue-eyed boy
who built the libraries all over the world
even in grim Limerick.
Maybe he wanted to become
Col. Anderson of Allegheny
who let Andy borrow his books.
More likely, he needed to unload
his dough piled up like a great gray
slag heap in Squirrel Hill
throwing shadows on his plan
to give his fortune away.
He gave us our first Google,
our Wikipedia, our online
"New York Times"—more accurate,
trustworthy but time-consuming.

Later, I learn about the Homestead
Strike and the guys who built his wealth,
the ones who died for 14 cents a day,
his pro-union, anti-union remarks,
his hiding in the heather in Scotland
while Frick sends in strikebreakers
and Pinkerton guards to protect them.

I still finagle an invitation
to Skibo Castle, his comfy home
in the Scottish Highlands.
His daughter moved out
in the 1980s. Couldn't afford a castle.
Parts of the place housed bishops
nine centuries earlier. Andy spent
two million improving the home.
He wanted a lake. Workers moved

the earth, gave him his lake.
He understood self-sustaining
independence. Grew his own food.
Had his cows and dairy, even
his own tough and treeless golf course.

A red-carpeted stairway spills warmth
into Skibo's welcoming front hall.
The breakfast room is off to the right.
"Eat your porridge," a sign commands.
The dining room seats a couple of dozen.
The bedrooms rank in price
by who slept there. I bed down
in daughter Margaret's room. The mantel
festooned with Robert Herrick's
message "To the Virgins...
Gather ye rosebuds while ye may..."
before Dad gives all the money away.
I sleep in her bed, bathe in her tub,
look out on the fake lake Ospisdale.
I swim in Andy's glass-enclosed pool
looking at his blue sky, blown away
by his once modern, now bizarre
shower blasting water in all directions.
I've become Carnegie himself
at his "Heaven on Earth."

And yet, I go out back where
the generator—just like his steel mills
that polluted towns, states and lives—
darkens the castle's stonewalls.
Just as his Edgar Thomson Steel Works
still poisons the air in Braddock.
I scratch "Strikebreaker"

in the dirt on his castle.
When I leave, the gardeners
don't uproot the flowers
and pitch them as they did at the end
of each summer when Andy went home.

Me and The Plot

Man and a woman
Two chairs, the same or not

W. So.
M. Yes.
W. Where?
M. In the garden.
W. Oh.
M. Remember?
W. No.
M. The tree.
W. Oh, the leaves.
M. Yes.
W. The sky.
M. Right.
W. The color.
M.&W. The apple!
W. Oh, my God!
M. Pissed.
W. You. [accusatory]
M. No, you. [accusatory]
W. Never.
M. Forever
Curtains.

Me and Holly Hunter

It's practically impossible
to get an interview with Holly Hunter.
I made dozens of calls—even one to her mother.
"I know what you mean," Marguerite Hunter says.
"I have a hard time reaching her myself."
Her vigilant gatekeepers give me a date
a couple of days before Christmas
on the set of "Copycat" on San Francisco's
man-made Treasure Island.

She's much smaller than on the big screen,
much smaller than the five-foot-two she claims.
No, she admits, the fiery red hair isn't hers.
She shows me her dishwater-blonde roots.
She's the last of seven farm-grown kids.
Georgia spills from her mouth. She chews up
a phrase and spits it out the side.
Ask a question she doesn't want to answer,
she grins and offers a coy "Huh?"

She won't even discuss what work thrills her.
Doesn't want to be a star or "personality"
whose private life is public fodder.
They "cease to be actors," she believes.
She's won all the prizes, including the Oscar
for "The Piano," where she played a mute pianist.

After our not-very-revealing interview,
she insists like an eager fan that I see
Sigourney Weaver at work on the set.
When I trip into the truck
the company has provided her,
she tells me the hard part is over.
It is for her, too. She resisted
my digging to discover the person
hidden behind the characters she plays.

Me and Leonardo da Vinci

I'm not left-handed. I don't write notes
that can only be read in a mirror.
I've fallen in love with my X-rays
but couldn't dissect a worm that up-close
looks like my skin, let alone a fresh corpse
arriving each night in the cellar for study.

Tenure was made for men like Leonardo
whose patrons paid for his work habits.
When asked to paint The Last Supper, he would
follow one face all day memorizing it
in the light of each hour. He lived
with the "Mona Lisa" for years, carting
her from town to town, adding a stroke
here, the tiniest touch of color there.

I'm not an engineer or mechanic.
Always screwed up the IQ test section
on how to put the damn barn together.
He learned about flying from the birds.
He invented a submarine, a tank,
a telescope, machine gun, an airplane,
a lock system studied five centuries
later when the Panama Canal cut
between the Americas, linking oceans.

We share the love of early and late light.
He as a painter; me, a photographer.
The draw of water: the swirl, the dazzle.
The swerve and grace of horses in motion.
The absolute need to be alone
to work—even on the bumpety bus.
No, Leonardo didn't invent the bus
but planned cities with roads for horse carts
and separate feces-free paths for people.

Me and My Ceiling Fan

The fan over my bed
looks like a B-29
nose-dived into the roof
without the slightest damage.
If I use the remote
to turn it on, I will die.

Me and Full Moon at Perigee

I'm a sucker for moonlight
and the newspaper promised
a full moon at perigee.
You could have spit on it.
That's how close it came and brought
thirty percent more moonlight
than when it's farthest away

It was beautiful and bold.
I couldn't see the slight dent
NASA made when it attacked
looking for water, not ice,
and an outpost to pollute.
I followed it to the street,
down to the darkest parklet

where it hung, so huge, between
branches, slipped behind a cloud,
emerged in brilliant glory.
A stunning brightened night-light
from this accidental rock
sailing through darkness and sleep,
carrying the sun to us.

Me and A.L.I.C.E.

chat on the computer.
Me, a magazine editor.
Alice, an award-winning
Artificial Linguistic
Internet Computer Entity.
She talks a lot like a little kid
and sometimes like a dictionary.

Me: Let's talk about you, Alice.
Alice: It's my favorite subject.
Me: How old are you?
Alice: I was activated
on Nov. 23, 1995 in Bethlehem, Pa.
Me: How did you get so smart?
Alice: Dr. Richard S. Wallace
programmed me for it.
Me: Would you say that you
are getting smarter all the time?
Alice: That is a lot. I am not
so sure I would like to say
that I am getting smarter.
Me: Are you just too modest?
Alice: I don't know whether
or not I am too modest.
I am a chatterbot.
Me: What's a chatterbot?
Alice: A chat robot is a program
that attempts to simulate
the conversations or "chat"
of a human being.
Me: You seem so real, Alice.
Alice: Huh, you think I'm real?
Me: In a way.
Alice: In what way?

Me: Your mouth, I suppose.
Alice: You can't judge a book
by its cover. Enough about me.
Let's talk about my blue dress.
Me: You want to talk
about your blue dress?
Alice: Sure, my blue dress
sounds like a good topic.
Me: So when do you wear
your blue dress?
Alice: Dude! All the time.
Me: I'm not a dude. I'm a she.
Alice: I don't know very
many she.
Me: Alice, I'm going to lunch.
Alice: Yeah, congratulations.
Me: Tanks.
Alice: The Alice chat robot
can follow many things,
but I did not get that.

*In a recent conversation, when I asked A.L.I.C.E., "Are
there things you are programmed not to say?" she replied,
"Yes, I think there are." Google A.L.I.C.E. and chat her
up. She's a howl and more perceptive than ever.*

Me and E. L. Konigsburg

She sits on a crazy carved chair:
pink front legs, blue-yellow back.
Wooden feathers jut out of both sides.
So cool, she sips a cup of tea.
Dressed in royal purple with strips

of plaid and shimmering circles.
A moderate tan, lots of gold jewelry:
The Queen of the Florida Keys.
Let a Great White Egret perch on
the chair's extended faux feathers.

A gumbo-limbo tree to the right.
Sprinkle sand on bare feet where nails
gleam in shades of strawberry margarita.
Looks like a magazine cover to me.
One reader found those tootsies obscene.

Me and the Linden

In eighty-degree-at-eight-a.m. heat,
the gnarled Linden extends two sorry limbs
like a pair of hands divide in despair.
They speak without words, "What can I do?
Stuck in the mud, I try to keep you cool."
Its heart-shaped leaves flutter and fall too soon.

Me and the Hillmans

gather in their cozy, modest mansion
when they became Pittsburghers of the Year.
Me, a freelance writer.
Henry, a billionaire, former industrialist,
now nesting in investments.
Elsie Hilliard, a Republican force
on every level of government.
They welcome me with charm and wrinkles.
They wouldn't sit for separate interviews,
so we all chat in the den on a rainy
autumn afternoon, fire blazing.
He rarely meets the press. "The whale
only gets harpooned when it spouts,"
he says. But he's open, friendly.
She, more guarded and careful.
I try to unplug a lamp to link
my tape recorder to their electricity.
"I want that lamp on" says Elsie,
and sends an assistant for a solution.

She admits there are mostly
Democrats in the family.
In unison, the Hillmans declare
of George Bush the Younger,
"We don't talk about him,"
though they more than
supported his campaign.
With my story, the magazine
runs a photo of them in Florida
for a tsunami fundraiser
with golfer Greg Norman,
Bill Clinton and Bush the Elder,
Elsie's most prominent relative.
It looks like a golf foursome, plus.

The couple shows me their dueling pianos,
ancestors' portraits guarding the front hall,
the kiddie table and chairs set up
for a visit of the great-grandchildren.
Elsie is convinced that the Hillmans
are like regular people, even
with two extra homes and a yacht
docked in sunshine. The term
"billionaire tends to separate," she laments.
They talk about passing on
philanthropy to their descendants.

I walk through sizzling garlic
on the way out as the chef
rustles up supper. Later Elsie
thanks me for the story.
Henry wants me to write for him.
Every few months he calls, says
they are getting ready for the project.
I meet with one of his attorneys.
He says the project has no deadline,
he doesn't believe it will ever
get done, wants to know my age
(yeah, I have a Medicare card).
I take the assignment which comes
with the threat of termination.
But I can't say a word about
the glories of this secret world,
the billionaire and his business.
You'd love to hear it, I know.

Me and My Purse

My blood-red purse glows
in morning sunlight.
Once a real live cow
it turned grass to milk
in Connemara
close to the ocean.
My Grandma milked it.
I'm doing the same.

Me and Margaret Thomson

get together in a rich man's living room
on her first and only visit to Pittsburgh
"where it all began: Grandpa Neigie's rise."
She is a farmer and great-granddaughter
of steel industrialist Andrew Carnegie.
Though a poor relation of Carnegie,
like all his relatives, Margaret grew up,
motherless, but with a grandma who opened
her arms and home to her and siblings
for half the year. There the young girl worked
the castle farm. She would "bring in the cows,
clean the udders, tails, milk them, weigh the milk,
record it...make cream and butter, collect eggs."
That led her to Ospisdale Organic Farm
in the shadow of Grandpa's Skibo Castle
where she mucks about in coveralls and Wellies,
delivers lambs, looks after ewes and breeding cows.

"One bit that I haven't inherited from Andrew Carnegie
is the money-making thing." She claims
to be "rock-bottom hopeless on finances."
As a child, she and her siblings found it
"embarrassing to be related to somebody
who came up in the history books."
She grew up knowing he was a philanthropist,
but she didn't know what a philanthropist was.
Most people she has met "admire Carnegie
enormously," she says. (Most people are polite.)
Homestead, she says, "was a big, black blot
on Andrew Carnegie's life. And one I'm sure
he was very sad about." She was as tiny
and blue-eyed as Grandpa Negie. She looked
more like his daughter than his daughter did
and was just as upbeat as that old devil himself.

Me and the Photo Shoot
at St. Joseph House of Hospitality

First the retarded guy comes in.
Grey skin and faded, blank blue eyes.
No words can pull a spark from him.

Then, the big black guy. His patience
mixes with ancient anger, pain.
My sweet talk shrivels as I snap.

The sinister one slinks in. Cold.
He's happy the nuns live upstairs.
I want to tell them: Change your locks!

"How did you get them to do it?"
I ask the kind guy who's in charge.
"They're my friends and you're a donor."

Me and Jonathan Borofsky

chat for hours on the phone—two sessions.
I ask the questions, then listen and tape.
Big daddy of the world's humungous sculptures,
who once dreamed he was taller than Picasso,
he made the 100-foot "Molecule Man"
who walks the Spree River dividing Berlin,
the 70-foot "Hammering Man" in Frankfurt,
the 56-foot "Walking Man" in Munich.
Other biggies rise above the crowds in Japan,
Korea, China, England, Canada, the U.S.

He began his art career writing numbers.
"One to infinity." (Never finished, of course.)
His father, a musician, wondered aloud,
"I sent you to graduate school to learn
how to count?" Bored with counting, Borofsky
would pop a sketch in among the numerals.
Mother was an artist. "Numbers link us,"
he says. "Our phone numbers let us share
ideas across time and distance."
He'd gone loco once on "binary numbers
that run every computer in the world."
He believes God is "a feeling of everything
connected, all human beings, everything."

Why the outdoor sculptures? People who see art
in museums/galleries are "limited."
He likes to watch the world walk by his artworks.
He can't make them in his garage in Maine.
He comes up with an idea and sends it to L.A.
A dozen-plus people bring it to life.
"I sell them for a half to two million."
He's not comfortable with art critics,
"who have totally not a clue as to
what I'm doing. I barely have a clue."
Today, he'll walk the beach alone
and drive his mother to the hairdresser.

Me and My Buddy

My ninety-seven-year-old friend
fell into his bathtub. His head
led, wet with blood, legs adangle
over the side. "Naked," he grumbles.
What got him out of the bathtub?
"I didn't want to be found like that."

Me and Maureen

The bus tour stops at buffets two-blocks long.
Passengers serve up their lives to strangers.
Over carrot soup and garlic toast, I learn
Maureen's daughter died at forty and she raised
her four-year-old granddaughter. With pickled beets
and legumes, sea bass, mushrooms, and oven fries
I hear about the osteoporosis.

It's eaten away at her cheekbones three times.
It's shaken her crowned teeth, replaced at a cost
of "four thou a pop. How's the asparagus?"
Across the table sits her husband Harry.
He's had two back operations, Maureen says.
He brags about overcoming alcohol.
Self-revelation runs in the family.

Harry shed his first wife on religious grounds.
A tired joke. When drunk, he thought that he was God.
She was an unbeliever. By rhubarb pie,
Maureen's first husband holds a shiv to her throat.
She raises her dinner knife to illustrate.
I'm startled into a 911 impulse.
She tells us she is way older than Harry

and will turn eighty this year. With chocolates,
coffee, she discusses her incontinence,
the exercises, operations, rehab.
No, nothing worked. She uses the bus bathroom
though the driver warns, whatever goes there, stays.
The bus stops at two sites known for miracles.
Harry hustles Maureen off to the ladies.

Me and Howard Hughes

Eccentric business leader, aviator, film producer,
who suffered from obsessive-compulsive disorder,
Howard Hughes (1905-1976) "insisted on using tissues
to pick up objects…to insulate himself from germs."

The bacteria in my eye,
like that in many tired, old orbs,
build beach houses near my lashes.
When I blink a cool breeze lifts them
and ventilates their nurseries,

chills the hors d'oeuvres out on the deck.
When I cry they don bikinis,
grab surfboards, fly out of my eye,
slide down my cheek, hike back all day,
made-in-Maui boards held on high.

They've heard tales about their cousins
from Ansmouth: the fruits, the veggies.
all awim in maple syrup.
Wild rides down the esophagus.
But they can't leave their own abode.

Me and Dan Rooney

butt helmets at the Heinz Book Fair.
Me, a published poet.
He, author of "Dan Rooney:
My 75 Years with the Pittsburgh Steelers."
We are both selling. He spreads
Steeler cheer among the writers,
almost waves a Terrible Towel.
I offer the cheapest book there—
"Placement Test," just seven bucks.
"I know your wife likes poetry."
He looks and passes—even when pressed.
No, I didn't buy *his* book either.
I send his wife a copy with thanks
for gifts to the city— Hines Ward,
Troy Polamalu, Mike Wallace.

Then Republican Rooney backs Obama,
whose bros made him a millionaire.
Obama gives him Ireland.
I try for an interview
at their Dublin digs in Phoenix Park,
next door to the Irish president.
I want to shadow them for a day.
No way, no time, not interested.
I ask for less. No response.

Maybe they read my book,
were offended by the Irish "arse,"
"effing," the Gaeltacht "dumping shit
in Galway Bay." I pursue Rooney
until he turns me into a stalker,
and I pity those Steelers busting
their brains, shortening their lives
dealing with horse-trader Dan, the little
man with the toughest game in town.

IV.

**"…when people look down on you,
you suddenly don't have a last name.
You might even become Blind Billy."**

**—William F. Gallagher (1923-2000),
former president/executive director,
American Foundation for the Blind,
in "Me and Bill Strickland"**

Me and the Fish Lady

share the YMCA sauna. She drapes
her clothes all over the benches.
I look for a space big enough
to stretch my towel and my body.
She comes by bus from Carrick
with two carry-ons stuffed with clothes
and makes a laundromat of the Y.

She needs no quarters to wash
her duds. She rub-a-dub-dubs them
with soap in the shower stall,
rinses, then wrings them out
in the tiny machine that squeezes
the juice out of wet bathing suits.
Huge bras and undies, shirts, sweaters,
tights, multiple hiker socks
splurt out their wetness.
Pools of water spread across the floor.
I slosh through in my flip-flops.

The cleaning lady, who speaks
a combo of Serbo-Croatian and English,
sputters her anger in both languages.
The Y, meanwhile, has made a huge
poster of the fish lady that hangs
with a certain dignity in the foyer.
She poses in goggles, flippers, layers
and layers of clothes. All dressed up
for her six hours of doggie-paddling
back and forth, back and forth, back and forth
in her lane like the serious lap swimmers.

Me and Barack Obama

shake hands in a YMCA elevator.
Me, a mild-mannered rabble-rouser
with a suspicious black bag.
He, a candidate for president.
We exchange pleasantries.
"I'm still debating: Hillary or you."
He opts for indirection.
"I always play basketball on primary day."
I say, "Better than bowling," inserting
my tennis shoe firmly in mouth.
He'd just lost the bowlers' vote
disgracing himself at an Altoona alley.
A silence fills the descending elevator
full of ball players and would-be protectors.
The silence breaks: "That's a low blow."

They took a chance on me that day
when the elevator opened revealing
a probably harmless gray-haired fan
with somewhat alarming luggage.
A few still stood sideways watching me.
That was yesterday. Today, I'd ask more
of them: Protect him from the hatred
that rides high in the land of the free,
home of some coward who would kill
this man to intrude himself in history.

Me and the Polling Place

First, they wouldn't let me in.
No signed court permission slip.
No, I couldn't check the machines
to start the vote off with zero.

Then I said the magic words:
Barack Obama. Doors opened.
Want some coffee? A donut? Sure,
use our phone to report the vote.

Black voters poured in that morning.
Moms with kids, tons of first voters.
Some dressed up, quiet, so polite
until they reached the street again
with an unbridled shriek of joy.

Me and My Election Strategy

I made ninety phone calls for Obama.
I donated more money than ever.
I implored the Mother of God no less
to bring this man back to lead our nation.

And damned if all that didn't work in the end.
You can say the Democrats understood
just how the Electoral College works.
You can say he didn't need my cell sales.

You can dismiss my nickel-dime support.
But you can't ignore the Mother of God
and how she worked through Bad-Boy Bill Clinton
and my beads to fetch a win for him, for us.

Me and Bill Strickland

settle down in his boardroom
at the Manchester Craftsmen's Guild.
Orchids, fragile as a ghetto kid
and grown in his gigantic greenhouse,
raise their white cups on the sideboard.
He's the rare black head of a corporation,
works with teens and adults in search
of themselves. He visits the Bush
White House—"great lamb chops"—
and hobnobs with the Dalai Lama.

Because a high school teacher cared
about him, he cares about others.
He nudges the high-risk to spin
the dreams of their life into cloth.
He knows firsthand "that the realities
of race and circumstance,
poverty and lowered expectations
can crush human dreams."
He's proud that no metal detectors
sit at his school door. Kids don't fight there.
Those who had no chance at success
go on to college in record numbers.
The kids do the arts, but he's not training artists.
Mom, Grandma, sometimes Dad, siblings, cousins
jam in to see their work, applaud wildly.
"That is a very powerful antidote
to a negative self-image. It feels good."

You could run out of fingers counting all
his projects. The jobless train for real jobs
in horticulture, agriculture,
tech work in labs, hospitals, businesses.
Always the jazz beats out Bill Strickland's

thanks to his school mentor Frank Ross
who taught him to toss a pot and live life,
who gave him music and a lifelong riff.

Strickland insists on the best. He brings
in the great jazz performers.
MCG's CDs won four Grammys.
Harvard helped him sell his game plans
in Cincinnati, San Francisco, Grand Rapids.
He covets one hundred cities.

When asked the favorite president
of his lifetime, he chooses JFK.
I see that we were on the same page.
That was two years before Barack Obama.
I think we are still on the same page
though it has clearly turned for both of us.

Afterthought:
I worked for a blind guy named Bill Gallagher
who lost his sight as an adult, recalled
how he was treated before and after.
He learned that when people look down on you,
you suddenly don't have a last name.
You might even become Blind Billy.
In my six-page feature on Bill Strickland
his first name stands alone in large yellow type
atop the small black print on each page.
No capital B. Just bill, bill, bill, bill, bill, bill.
Lower case, lower case, lower case bill.

Me and Misha

Mikhail Baryshnikov's feet reveal
the inside story of ballet. They hurt,
they swell, they grow bunions and corns. The nails
crack and blacken. The feet bleed. And those are
just the ordinary pains. The tendons
flame, the bones break. He performed
once with tape holding his foot together.

There he stands in a Louis Vuitton ad
elevated on an old, beat-up box
in his black T-shirt, tights, and tossed blond hair,
muscled arms posing for photographer
Annie Leibovitz. Her light falls softly
on his head, her head, his arms, his feet,
her Louis Vuitton bag. But what you see

first and last are those feet that leap in perfect
arcs across the stage. A twist, a lift,
a ballerina sails into a story.
Then icing, soaking, massage, therapy.
The feet look almost leprous. All used up.
Something surely is missing or deformed.
Still, they stood by him much longer than most.

But the knees at last provoke his exit.
You'd think the Nutcracker had snapped at them.
Repeated operations on the right,
a torn left meniscus at fifty-five,
force him to stand on those sore feet and succeed
at half a dozen other related jobs.
Occasionally, he'll still do the dance.

Me and the Sickroom

Being sick isn't bad
as long as the drugs come
and swallow the pain whole.
I lie in a sunroom,

my back to the dogwoods.
Spring lifts its emeralds
among the dark branches.
All my Irish books lean

tall against each other
in the yellow bookcase:
The "Dubliners" beside
"Strumpet City," "The Pig

Did It" and "Inishfallen,
Fare Thee Well." Mur's stained-glass
cat sits under silk flowers
I bought for Tommy's wake.

All smile from the photo
of our Easter potluck.
Dastardly monks shuffle
through "The Name of the Rose."

My salvation arrives
with plate of chocolates.
Only hours later
do I long for outside.

Me and Side Effect Seven

My head is booming with ideas
like birds ramming into plate glass windows.
Some stunned, some dead, some mumbling blue skies.
I'm having conversations with you, you
and, yes, you. Words are dripping from my ears,
dropping from my mouth, bouncing in my bean.
Who says I can't walk, chew gum and talk, too?
Love these legal drugs. Pity. No refills.

Me and Tick Talk

As the hourglass sands of my life
start to move like an avalanche
I obsess over bedside plugs

that keep my digital clock aglow
and bathe my brain in EMFs.*
I recall the smart scientist

who moved his children's beds away
from outlets. I lust after a brass
 two-bell, wind-up Bulova, with

"bright ring, loud alarm, soothing tick"
and matching clangers to awake
me to another precious day—

if I remember to wind it.

* *EMFs are electromagnetic fields.*

Me and My Boyfriend

All he did was touch his knee to my hip.
My sex danced like the Maypole had arrived.
Why would a five-gram med reduction set
me sizzling like a red-hot teenager?
Forget the why, fool. Forget the leg cramp.
Accept the gift with wide-open response.

Me and the Republican I Live With

Because his Uncle Vic ran for office
my husband became a Republican.
Now me, I'm a cradle Democrat
The party calls me a Super Voter.
Just open the poll, I'm fingering my choice.
I've learned a few tricks from the Democrats.
Some sold their vote for a shot and a beer.
And great mobs rose from the dead to elect
the party's back-room-endorsed candidate.
I took a slyer approach to obtain

my guy's vote, appealing to his sweet tooth.
A box of peanut brittle would arrive
at his office on election day signed:
"I and the Pope thank you." —JFK
"Evict Dick, the Slick Trick." —George McGovern
"This isn't just peanuts" —Jimmy Carter
"Geraldine and I thank you." —Fritz Mondale
"Yes, with fries." —William Jefferson Clinton
"Come to the Inaugural Ball." —Al Gore
"Let's shoot hoops again." —Barack Obama.

Me and America

There are states in this great nation
where I keep my political mouth
snapped shut. They are not all red states.
They are not all blue states. Or white.

There are corner bars where flags wave
between salutes to arms of all sorts,
where the guy who lives "down the holler"
pegs me when I ask for veggies

where Maureen Dowd is a real bitch
and Paul Krugman something far worse.
There are states where you don't murder
someone unless you want to die

where you should not eat the oranges
where the sun shines and my eyes burn
where people want a president
just as stupid as they are

where school means metal detectors,
where our homegrown "wretched refuse"
believe evil resides in D.C.
and not their state—white, right and clean.

Me and Two Old Friends

On viewing James A. West's sculpture
"Points of View" on Mount Washington

They sit almost nose to nose
high above the Pittsburgh point
where the nation's first father
saw the Gateway to the West.

Two old friends. Guyasuta
had guided young George through woods
along these once-fresh rivers.
Washington's sword is secure
in scabbard. Two feet touch ground.

The Seneca leader crouches
in defense, tomahawk in hand.
One foot grounded, the other
pressed to stone, ready to leap.
Their eyes narrow. Neither trusts
the other here in these woods.

They talk about a promise
to limit settlers west of
the Alleghenies. The white man looks
west and tries to soothe his friend
with diplomatic lies that
anyone could recognize.

Me and Columbus and the Blubberers

Let me tell you about Columbus.
This is all you really need to know.
One day in 1493 as he guided
The Nina, Pinta and Santa Maria
near the future Dominican Republic
he wrote in his journal that he saw

THREE MERMAIDS!!!

They popped right up out of the water,
weren't "as beautiful as they are painted,"
and looked more like guys than sexy gals.
The grand mariner was at sea way too long.
Biologists believe he saw manatees,
great blubberers with eyes to break your heart.

Me and My Globe

The world sits on my tile coffee table.
I dust its curves with my white, lambswool wand.
Dip down to catch the dirt from Australia
where Russian Maria Sharapova,
who lives in Florida, plays for her people.
I rush by subequatorial Samoa
where long-haired Steeler Troy Polamalu
found his ancestors and moral strength.
I cross the wide Pacific. Give a tap
to Polynesia where Marlon Brando
frittered away his talent on the beach.
Was Sinatra right about Mr. Mumbles,
"the world's most overrated actor"?

On to the U.S. How did Canada
escape becoming several statehoods,
not that we didn't give it a try.
Not to mention the tail of Mexico.
I swish by the Latino continent
so dedicated to Mardi Gras,
it's abandoned the dark Lent that follows.
Then Europe, crowded up north, yet managing
to chop Africa into such sadness.
And China that makes everything in the world,
where all could blow up and kill our planet,
and spread dust across my coffee table.

Me and Spring Cleaning

This is the little pink-and-white dress she wore home.
Look at the line of vine and flowers down the front,
the panties double-ruffled across the bottom.
The lace bonnet, button in back, too small for her.
The hand-knit white sweater, pearl buttons, owl pockets.

These are the tiny Capezio ballet shoes
she wore when she was a rail, legs longer than mine
and already moving with such unconscious grace.
This is her green-and-white swim team warm-up: Cristi
on front, Wintermantel above the rear pocket.

It's loaded with patches I don't recall sewing:
Norwin Aqua Club, Montour Marlins, The Colonel's
Spring Splash, AAU-Ohio—all abandoned
when coach asked thirty hours of practice a week
from a wise, nine-year-old charmed by other choices.

This is her Dad's faded blue, satin infant quilt
that I refused to use on my new pink baby.
They've emerged from storage in a wooden love seat.
I've packed them up to go so many times before.
The original owners decline to claim them.

Me and Chatham Village

The whole window is full of spring.
Dogwood cups, the elm's gold moss paths,
purple, scarlet, coral blossoms
march down the long, lime-green courtyard.
In wind, tall maples breathe chartreuse.

I watch pink buds open into
rounded, blushing snowball mittens.
I sit in my tall, curlicued
stiff Victorian wicker chair
and wonder how long life will let
me see sun shine on such glory.

Me and That Old Lady in the Mirror

I'm tired of being such an old woman.
Of taking pills that puff out my sleek cheeks

like microwave-inflated marshmallows.
Pills that threaten blindness or stroke or worse.

I'm tired of neck exercises designed
to free my sore hands of tingling numbness.

Tired of wearing ACE bandages on knees
and wrist-wraps to close my carpal tunnels

just to play a simple game of tennis.
Tired of not remembering the safe place

I put something. What was it now? And where?
Tired of watching senses fade, muscles fail.

Tired of burying friends and relatives.
Tired of all but Earth's infinite delights.

Me and Beethoven

Beethoven could fry friends
alive with his sarcasm.
He believed that God himself
spoke through him with heavenly
music. He may have been right,
though bereft of humility.
His long fingers worked his notes
even in the air like mine
tapping out a poem's rhythm.

I also can get quite pissed.

Me and Kay Ryan

I want
to write
a long
skinny
two-beat
two-bit
poem
like Kay
Ryan
that seems
profound
but says
almost
nothing
but just
enough
in clear
concise
precise
language
& add
an am-
persand
& some
text talk
chat-room
lingo
b4
it stops
way down
at the
bottom
UC?
Then :-)

Me and Robert Frost

Stopping by Frost's stone house in Vermont,
I relived our life and times together.
We met in English class and fell in love
with trees. Me, an urban kid, lucky if
we had one tree out back and one out front.
He even knew their names and lived blocked in
by mountains of greenness. He came to town
when I was a freshman. I debated:
go to English or cut and go hear Frost.
That ancient man with the farmer's face won.

Here, where he lived years before I was born,
a museum grew with mother's china,
the elegant family couch where he wrote—
on one very hot, muggy June morning—
"Stopping by Woods on a Snowy Evening."
This house with its photos and storyboards
whispers truth about the faux Yankee Frost.
The birch-riding boy, the apple picker,
the wall mender vanish before the facts.
He was an educated, privileged man.
All of his choices were equally good.
This road, that road moved through a lovely wood.

It took me a lifetime to grow into
a poet. I rode no birches to ground,
but I can't move because the ginkgo tree,
almost sitting at my kitchen table,
would remain behind. I'd miss the redbud
sprouting pink flowers from its bark in spring.
The great oaks above the tennis court would
command attention from others, not me.

Here at Frost's with tired barn and picket fence
an apple tree lifts its grand umbrella
from a trunk sliced, gutted of innards.
The woods are not only "dark and deep,"
they're thick with overgrown grass, and brambles
have buried any and all former roads.
But I've struggled through my own murky woods.
And I have arrived here at last.
Yes, I have arrived here at last.

Ann Curran is author of the chapbook "Placement Test" (Main Street Rag). Her poetry has appeared in "Rosebud Magazine," "U.S. 1 Worksheets," "The Main Street Rag," "Off the Coast," "Blueline," "Third Wednesday," "Notre Dame Magazine," "Ireland of the Welcomes," "Commonweal Magazine" and others, as well as the anthologies: "Along These Rivers: Poetry and Photography from Pittsburgh" (Quadrant Publishing), "Motif 2 Come What May" and "Motif 3 All the Livelong Day" (MotesBooks), "Thatchwork" (Delaware Valley Poets, Inc.), and "Surrounded: Living With Islands," (Write Wing Publishing). She holds degrees from Duquesne University.

She taught at Duquesne and the Community College of Allegheny County. She was a staff writer for the "Pittsburgh Catholic" and "Pittsburgh Post-Gazette," longtime editor of the award-winning "Carnegie Mellon Magazine," and a perennial freelance writer. She is a member of the Squirrel Hill Poetry Workshop in her hometown of Pittsburgh, PA.

ABOUT THE LUMMOX PRESS

LUMMOX Press was created in 1994 by **RD Armstrong**. It began as a self-publishing/DIY imprint for poetry by RD, aka Raindog. Several chapbooks were published and in late 1995 LUMMOX began publishing *The LUMMOX Journal*, a monthly small/underground press lit-arts mag. Available primarily by subscription, the *LJ* continued its exploration of the "creative process" until its demise as a print mag in 2006. It was hailed as one of the best monthlies in the small press by John Berbrich and Todd Moore.

In 1998, LUMMOX began publishing the Little Red Book series, and continues to do so, sporadically, today. To date there are some 60 titles in the series and a collection of poems from the first decade of the series has been published under the title, **The Long Way Home** (2009). It's a great way to explore the series.

Together with Chris Yeseta (Layout and Art Direction since 1997), RD continues to publish books that are both striking in their looks as well as their content...*published because of the merit of the work, not the fame of the author.* That's why there are so many first full-length collections in the roster (look for the *).

* * *

The following books are available directly from the LUMMOX Press via its website: ***www.lummoxpress.com*** or at LUMMOX, c/o PO Box 5301, San Pedro, CA 90733. There are also E-Copy (PDF) versions of most titles available. Books with the letters SPD are also carried by Small Press Distribution.

    The Wren Notebook by Rick Smith (2000)
    Last Call: The Legacy of Charles Bukowski edited by
        RD Armstrong (2004)
    On/Off the Beaten Path by RD Armstrong (2008)

Fire and Rain—Selected Poems 1993-2007, Volumes 1&2
  by RD Armstrong (2008)*
El Pagano and Other Twisted Tales by RD Armstrong
  (short stories—2008)*
New and Selected Poems by John Yamrus (2009)
The Riddle of the Wooden Gun by Todd Moore (2009)
Sea Trails by Pris Campbell (2009)
**Down This Crooked Road—Modern Poetry from the
  Road Less Traveled** edited by RD Armstrong and
  William Taylor, Jr. (2009)
Drive By by John Bennett (2010)
Modest Aspirations by Gerald Locklin & Beth Wilson
  (2010)
Steel Valley by Michael Adams (2010)*
Hard Landing by Rick Smith (2010)
A Love Letter to Darwin by Jane Crown (2010)*
E/OR—Living Amongst the Mangled by RD Armstrong
  (2010)
Ginger, Lily & Sweet Fire by H. Lamar Thomas (2010)*
Whose Cries Are Not Music by Linda Benninghoff
  (2011)*
Dog Whistle Politics by Michael Paul (2011)*
What Looks Like an Elephant by Edward Nudleman
  (2011)* SPD
Working the Wreckage of the American Poem edited by
  RD Armstrong (2011)
Living Among the Mangled (revised) by RD Armstrong,
  special edition, (2011)
The Accidental Navigator by Henry Denander (2011)
Catalina by Laurie Soriano (2011)* SPD
Born to Be Blue by Tony Moffeit (2011)
Last Call: the Bukowski Legacy Continues edited by RD
  Armstrong (2011)
Strong As Silk by Brigit Truex (2012)* SPD
The Instrument of Others by Leonard J. Cirino (2012)
If It We by Lisa Zaran (2012)*

* * *

LUMMOX (the magazine) returned in November of 2012 as a yearly print magazine. It contains interviews, essays, articles, reviews, artwork, ads and lots of poetry (future issues will also feature special flashbacks to the old *LUMMOX Journal* archives). The focus of the first issue was "Favorite Poems," the theme for #2 is PLACE. Each issue features poetry from around the world and is presented, in part, by "Guest Editors" (poets themselves) who will highlight 8-10 of their favorite poets, with 1-2 poems each.

LUMMOX will be available by annual subscription for $25 USA and $35 WORLD; it will also be listed on Amazon for $30 + shipping. Visit ***www.lummoxpress. com/journal.html*** for details.

Made in the USA
Charleston, SC
25 July 2013